Rainy Days on the Farm

Cover image by Lesle Lewis

Published in the United States by

Fence Books
110 Union Street
Second Floor
Hudson NY 12534

www.fenceportal.org
518-567-7006

This book was designed by Rebecca Wolff
printed by Versa Press www.versapress.com
and distributed by Small Press Distribution www.spd.org
and Consortium Book Sales and Distribution www.cbsd.com.

Library of Congress Control Number: 2019950667

Lewis, Lesle (1952–)
Rainy Days on the Farm / Lesle Lewis
winner of the Ottoline Prize

ISBN 13: 978-1-9443801-4-4

First Edition
10 9 8 7 6 5 4 3 2

Fence Books are published with the support of all Friends and Members
of Fence, and the New York State Council on the Arts and the National
Endowment for the Arts, as well as the Whiting Foundation.

Rainy Days on the Farm

LESLE LEWIS

THE OTTOLINE PRIZE

HUDSON   NEW YORK

Contents

Yesterday was yesterday.

We climbed on cameras.

Our cigarette ashes made castles.

We aligned the facts with the outcomes.

We were in a higher state from which we would descend.

Worlds bloomed and crumbled with echoes of devastation and privilege and fairies and pigs and pumpkins and a man under a thinking sign.

Sun rays slid through the stacks.

I was a breeze with a straight back with you, my brother, in the gladness of these rooms with chandeliers, rot, and excess.

We are fools.

I leave some heartache and a candy for you on the counter.

"So be it" you say as if you expect it won't be.

It's like pain, but it's not.

Our heart valves are yellow.

Humans could stop loving themselves quite so much.

Our table legs could give way and the drinks spill and the glasses break.

Someday we might say, "We've worked on this."

Can this whole thing not be both right for you and right for me?

Every day is a self-improvement opportunity.

I'm not finished with my self until there's nothing wrong with it.

It's easier to be good away from you.

It's easier to get my decorum right.

Our world is poor and needy.

The fix is slow.

Our Problems

1

Yesterday you were saying "help me," and I didn't understand.

Now I get it; your art is a way to have other problems.

So I embrace your shack and the time we spend there, your paint fires, your pet ducks, and any love that's transferred between us.

You also get paid to be blue sometimes.

You're like a communal public weeping, a countermonument in our city park.

2

The Vernal Pool Association encourages vernal pool certification for vernal pool protection.

The pool is lovely in the rain.

Cows stand in the pool to cool themselves and drop dung.

If you pour hot coffee into a cup of ice, you'll have what you want.

This is what summer looks like.

Let your ambition lie low.

If you worry about the money, I'll worry about the food.

3

At the Center for the Treatment and Study of Anxiety, the sound of the accelerating expansion of the universe continues.

If you struggle with your system, it may be that your system is too simple to be accurate.

Reconsolidate.

Erase yourself.

The tenses are only one way to systemize it.

What if I can't go for walks with you so I can't go for walks?

What if overloads of non-narrative informational detail become bolder?

Receding lines converge at the center of vision if they do not bend or curve, but how badly we want them to bend and curve!

Birdsong comes from birdsong-making machines and breath comes from breath-making machines.

I miss you every time I don't have to avoid you.

4

With two fingers, the good nurse touches you.

Your hair blows in your baby face.

If this memory comes back, ask it where it's been.

First, it was the sound of an apple rolling off the table and thudding on the floor, and then the sound of it rolling on the floor.

An Open Easy Door

If there is a couple.

If there is not.

One will die before the other.

If your little life.

A pentimento.

If you loved a banjo.

If you skipped the night.

If this is a post virtual reality crash.

If the text meanders.

Some carbon dioxide removal.

If these are flirtations.

What we share to be this "we."

Between one meal and another.

When we look into the mirror.

We are in a restaurant.

Whoever I look at, for a minute, I understand.

I have ideas.

If the rain.

A futile rain, a cement rain, an odd-shaped rain, a death rain, a newborn rain, a modest rain, a stopped rain, a coffee rain, a yellow rain.

Crows, babies.

If we are scarecrows in a garden by the sea.

If the house has a lake with a swan.

The swan has a lake.

We are less forlorn.

If the train whistle, the valley, the clouds.

If a white horse grazes in a distant field.

Exciting as can be.

Some part of this is like some part of that.

Your mind kind of goes where it goes until it sees something and stops.

You like what you like repeated.

There's no good way to tell you that you hardly matter to me, so I'll build you up, love you, love you, love you.

You're kind of a ghost.

You're holding a lamb.

She stands in the moonlight measuring moonshine.

"Ah," she says at 11:15, "to intend then is to hope, is it not?"

Her brain flips back and forth between concave and convex.

Three straight lines that meet each other at their end points and leave a space in the middle might be her family.

Fabric hung on the insides of glass squares that punctuate house walls might be her underthings.

Imaginary letters combined to make imaginary words might be her weekends.

But what if her adventure is no metaphor for bigger things and the bigger things are a metaphor for just this?

Rainy Days on the Farm

Day One

The science, the absence, the travels, the walls: we have to feed these things, all animals insufficient unto themselves.

Day Two

I called on you to be in your house in your head, to be in your apartment heart.

You promised me a letter, but then you died.

I am sorry that you died.

Day Three

Can I lift bricks all day, scrub pots, carry coal, nurse the sick?

To get up is to let the day have me.

To embrace irony is to see more or less clearly.

Day Four

We think it all rushes and blurs by, but we are the ones going,
and we are the ones with a problem.

Day Five

What everyone says about poetry is that its light is golden, its leaves
yellow, and the sound of it a butterfly running to town for milk.

This is a moment before something good will happen or something bad.

This is a footbridge, a tractor bridge more likely, into maybe the biggest cornfield in New Hampshire, so big you can never cross it and get to the river which is where you think you are going.

You are a little stoned and your truck is a little wrecked and you are a little late.

There are also littler children around and everyone seems in good spirits.

The sentence is an industrial building.

Four sentences are like four sleeping dogs or four visible wavelengths.

They have small hearts or gills.

They are impossible.

You find yourself at an unexpected age in an unexpected airport in an unexpected mood.

The sentence aims to be not proud, and to not judge harshly the conversations of the drunk.

The information with which we make choices and the floors we sleep on are sentences.

The sentence battles blindness to horizons, blindness to temperatures, empty space blindness, and line orientation blindness.

All the ways to be human: six bad and six good.

The sentence has pathetic, poetic bones.

This one is in the water.

She is an estate, a cottage, and an animal.

She is a fake box.

She is zero point zero.

One quarter of a pill for me and one and a half pills for her.

The sentence is a bump on itself.

Grazing the Bear

Duck, quilt, eye, misdemeanor, utensil, India.

Fresh, Egyptian, cement, irregular, full-time, Pepsi.

Fathom, equivocate, cardamon, ink, festoon, tumult.

Pester, linger, orchard, minus, hairline, graze.

Mania breaks.

My body in bed in the L shape is bad.

Bodilessness expands.

Through the dressing room window a pink and blue light up.

I know what I'm doing.

The upper floors of my box are finished.

Fragment plus fragment equals fragmentation and we can work harder with what we have left of what we have lost or what we have left of what we never had.

Raise the level of the fish pond, make a bread head, smile, whatever.

A white woman in a white snow rides a bus.

We're getting closer to the thing now that breaks the busyness around it: modern libraries and highways, then postmodern, then remodern, then done.

Out the window is a table.

Gladness is hard to trust like a tall dead tree and its tall dead reflection which does not strike deep into the water as it seems to.

Nip runs free.

Lightning sparks the field and fries the sound on the television.

And we know time is not real because if it were to stand still, it would still pass.

The darker, the lighter, the smaller, the richer the temporality.

Enter the adventures of Nip who is compact, thoughtful, attractive enough but shy, ungendered, tough, covered with hairy fur, with small whiskers and ears and not much of a snout, with small, usable hands.

Nip accepts affection or can do without.

Nip is blindsided by every midday.

Nip takes the ferry to Fishers Island.

Nip eats the pot cookie.

Nip drinks the coffee cold.

Today it is a different day.

We sleep in the king's bed in the queen's room.

Anything can mean anything.

Nip watches flowers grow and birds come and go on the patio.

Nip's sadness has staying power.

Nip's got wide categories and a bumpy planet head.

More than one thing is wrong.

Nip is wired for feeling.

Evolution seems a single-minded dampness, brightness, warmness, careless scrawl.

Nip is weak and thin, bleak and spare.

Nip suffers and enjoys comparisons with the sufferings and joys of others.

Cats become boars become cows become horses become people with a range of capacities.

Nip's name is Lark May Third Pink or Honesty Christmas.

We pack Nip's sadness project, validation of the project (which is not enough), and studies of the project into a suitcase and take it somewhere else.

We have a parade, a baby, a swim, a dinner, a concert, an ice cream.

Our rocks sweat, our cakes fail, our ceiling fans race, our children play water games.

We need breaks from the work and we can medicate or self-medicate or talk about it or not talk about it or study it endlessly or speak of it directly or keep it as background and lug it always.

Leaves hang from the hammock galaxy.

A scholar kills himself slowly and a critic more quickly.

The water moves the sheets.

Every time I think we're done, you continue speaking.

A toy in the pond greens.

Your failings become attractive.

They are catatonics.

They are hurdle-leapers.

In that bed and those boards, what does the B stand for?

The two sides of a lake?

For you then, because you're closer to death.

What happens to us?

Your voice saying my words.

The water moving the sheets.

Our worries melting in water, becoming more water.

That's how tired we are.

Midair

To learn is to lose what we thought we knew. We doze under just enough to wake not knowing where we are which is perfect.

⊙

It was a two second dream. Where were the king's clothes? You were wearing them.

⊙

I've always wanted to be allowed to walk through a room of people and say nothing, not hello, not how are you, not your work looks good. It's a new cabinet to be filled with perfumes and spices and bowls of pears and sweaters.

⊙

It's more what you think of yourself than what others think of you that makes a difference in the work you do, the life you lead, the food you cook, the pets you keep, the books you read, the places you travel, the hours you put in.

⊙

Did you say you're unwell? Every day you say so.

⊙

Never can you say, so ever may you try. Do more of it.

⊙

Trees don't grow from their bottoms, but they never did.

⊙

We are inclined to go visiting, but then we are shy, and we turn around. Our heads want to lie down.

⊙

The direct sun deshadows your shirts clothespinned to my underwear no longer clothespinned to the line.

⊙

You befriend a small white animal; you name it "my baby."

⊙

We spy an angel, a three-dimensional flatness aching in us to envision our efforts manifested.

⊙

"Are you meditating?" you ask me in English. No, I am sailing on a floral boat. I am primping in the Maggie tree.

⊙

Clearly, we would benefit from a change in medications. Clearly, we carry too much in our brain suitcases we unpack and pack again. We're usually ready early. Then we find something else to do, so ultimately, we're late.

⊙

Backwards go rarely lives and sentences water. Midair is where it happens. We become more and more inclusive until we can't but we still can.

⊙

The little boy knew he was not to go into the fish pool but when he threw the ball into the pool, the little girl had no qualms about wading in for it. The little boy threw the ball in for the little girl many times.

The front hugs the coast.

Can we bust out of the landscape and acquaint ourselves with another?

Remove the sentence from its context and let it be free to float, not true, not false?

What every statement leaves out is smooth and without hooks.

We hope something unbounded in us can meet itself like spring is a thing that can come.

If no one needs us, if it's hard, we feel how hard.

Boxes Curtains Invisible Product Hunger Carton

Citrus logical team guy slight dust

Elegant library mystic seventy eye pumpkin

Noon limit Caspian pollination mineral mink

Lake inn wedding coaster plaster melon

Ground Florence field wave cream heavy

Pond dollop absorb foam apothecary pistachio

Freeze violet ethereal verandah gargoyle siren

Sugar market break clear trim queen

Fern old ballet pine chalk blush

Cusp tame yacht magnet baseboard chrome

Stripe condition froth scoop haze transformation

Ground pear porthole tobacco cake zero

Apple bone clutter cigar south ceiling

Pearl cedar straw lamb winter powder

Lattice pollen edge Brazil linen undertow

Thigh crazy navy finish glide trooper

Perceptions … can be radically reshaped.

The message barrels in beginning with low-level perception
and moving forward via object recognition.

Anything might come next: furry pony legs, sorrow biscuits,
padded statues.

The slope of your shoulders makes me inexplicably anxious.

Whatever it is, it is the fluid that's needed for the future of whatever
walks out of the winter woods.

The rush of the gush becomes so much that nothing can flow the
other way.

Too much is too interesting too late at night.

When you take things apart to see how they work, that kind of works,
but you're not sure you can trust yourself.

You are under pressure to reconsider, you being me and me being you.

I take the train or we drive.

We have this huge amount of love for the unborn.

What it was about, it's not about.

A white haze suggests itself.

You no longer choose the daily assignments over acorns or the texture of heaven.

The woods are iced.

I'm down but not outstanding in the nasty weather or not you care.

What the It Does to the You

The day imploded.

On me.

When you were sober.

You figured out that the future has a lot.

Of roughness in it—guaranteed.

What you said to me was too soft.

To be believed and the lure of the Internet.

Into our lives like icicles' drips.

We have a wantingness.

For bright light to read by.

You are self-indulgent.

And I can't read you.

You are like a drink.

With no food or forgetting.

I dreamed that I dreamed.

You died on the couch.

I forgive you.

You are smoking.

And thinking.

I might, one might.

Put words on things other than paper.

Make heads of figures.

Out of a wider variety.

Of materials.

Like dog bones.

One might paint.

Leaves on the house.

Do I love myself?

For managing to be kind.

To those I judge.

Harshly.

Or hate myself.

For judging them?

You can't just do.

Anything to help.

It will all.

Go away.

Anyway.

I see small words.

On the horizon.

And I'm not.

Afraid to also be.

Ecstatic.

Via magnifying glass.

I zoom in.

On the small bridge.

Behind the trees.

In early spring.

In Holland.

A slight pinkness.

Touches the snow.

Or is it?

Just longing.

Do we touch?

Is it?

Cross-hatchings happening?

More installations.

At all times of the day?

The exceptions?

I can't find.

The poetry events.

Oh well.

B is for better.

Not a metaphor for.

But only a metaphor.

An unbearable love for.

People walking on earth.

Seahorses, pastries.

Hinged one to another.

With a boy in it.

The duck sees.

What the rabbit cannot.

The rabbit sees.

What the duck cannot.

It's an on-and-off.

Switch.

A matter of conjunctions.

Conjunction choice.

Not a matter.

Of general choice.

Fractions made.

Of letters.

D for David.

So much.

Comes at us.

E for eleven.

Summations.

Horticulturally speaking.

The letter was smoking.

Like a fish.

I don't know what to do with this machine.

I walked to your party through crusty crash-through snow the color of pig dung. The party was way too feel-goodish. I had to come back over bad roads. Then the power went out.

We walked your puppy in the field and you confessed your feelings. This time of year can be the worst for feelings. Competing streams of information hit each other. Situations outside ourselves pull down our shades of happiness.

This machine might work, but I don't know what it's good for.

No More Tables

In one dream there were a lot of pieces. In another, things went well.

⊙

If there is some "it" where "it" all works, we're not sure about it. In fact, no one even knows who did it.

⊙

There's always reconsidering to do, never mind considering in the first place. A long, long time waits for us to catch up.

⊙

You walk towards me, calling me, my name licking your lips, my tongue circling your briefcase. You control even your willingness not to control. That's the happy moment I am in. Retreating is our current forward motion.

⊙

Pessimistic conclusions fly through email tunnels and land hard upon us.

⊙

It wasn't until yesterday that we came together over beers and confessed our mutual appreciation of tiny framed objects, two Eastern, two Western.

⊙

I hesitate to be certain more and more and become more confident in this hesitation every day and how sweetly it relieves me of my skepticism every morning that I wake.

⊙

Clearly, underlining is bigger than what's being underlined.

⊙

The birds and bees and flowers and frogs, balms and lilies and breeze, in what we think of as a unique time, twitter and bloom.

⊙

These are the laws that help to free us and keep us from decision-making. Anyway, there are no more tables.

⊙

Line up the object words on the sentence shelf that's broken.

⊙

You have a little confidence which means some, but not a lot. You've got to criticize yourself first.

The woods are green with black holes.

People gather in a big white tent.

Trees rise to cover a sun.

Names separate things when they may not want to be separated.

We whisper to each other so we won't wake each other.

Will you please bring me coffee and prime my motorcycle and wash my pans?

Is the man in love done?

Ice

A question.

Of compositional detail.

And texture.

Good, tired.

Bitter unfriendly.

Doom and so on.

Generational shifts in.

Density of material.

People and trees under nets.

Restraint as weapon.

Memory as sandwich bread.

Digital time lapse.

The story of.

Woman, dog, otter.

Sea, jug.

Mist light.

And blue.

A four-legged zigzags.

Rain on snow.

Why are you.

Writing things down?

The shadow's cause.

Recycling.

Your wishes.

And capsules.

Alternatives.

Potatoes.

Objects on pedestals.

Action figures.

Landlines.

Cells.

You used to wait and wait.

For the sound of love.

When it opened the door.

Trouble.

Placing your body.

Your pony.

This morning.

The limits of sun.

On snowshoes.

We are not.

Going where.

You thought.

We were.

The finish.

Of safety.

Rolling.

Over.

Two Yeses

I dangle over the bed.

The pillow becomes my soft, puffy bicycle, and I ride off into the flatness.

The surrounding space is invisible.

I'm a hunk of space garbage and time is a big nothing.

Something else comes over the horizon and it does much better.

It's fierce and ox-like.

It adjusts me.

Its single cry is "Help."

I've got ten pages of what I call "doubt."

I am more comfortable letting breaths out to where there's plenty of room for them than taking them in to where I have only so much capacity.

I don't know where to sit.

I don't know what to do.

Where is there pleasure in turning around?

It's all light green damp woods, all yellow star flowers.

The warming speeds up and this is what we get.

What we call "fun" the first person says is language for the rate at which pain subsides.

The second person says, "There are no frogs on the Canary Islands."

The third person says, "Let it be dark so we can come to light," on what we call "our continent."

What we call "useful" the fourth person belittles.

We're stuck awake in this limited territory in which our wills are free to roam.

The rain is no argument for rain.

I know it's not all about us, at least not anymore.

It's a complicated and windy structure to think that a general freedom is equally important to a freedom from suffering.

Let's stop at the intersection which is the word "intersection," and look both ways because neither is obviously preferable.

An autopsy of the statue reveals half my obvious love for you.

It's exciting and it hurts.

I field trip down long stairways to the ocean.

I watch a school of giant fish come in.

I watch a man fight an elephant.

Children play in the rose-tinted waters.

Because I am disturbed by overlapping objects, I think I see boundary lines between them.

So what if uncategorized information overrules the categorized?

Let us love and to mate, oh!

Let's wrap around each other.

Our loving is a maroon square, then a very light blue non-shape, then moon-shaped.

We are not cautious.

"The causation is viewed as the emergence of the event from the state."

There is a general brightening and we snack on some Xanax.

The sea has sky over it.

Our breathing becomes complicated.

We return from our distant view nibbling at the birdseed of the fated flowers.

Composite physical objects with singular names rule over us.

We go downstairs to look for them.

We throw ourselves and our country balls against the walls.

We think this is definite, but it's sick-bed work and not definite at all.

The only town exactly like this one is this one and any other town can only be as close as we are.

We are not twins, have hardly a future, and we are terribly stormy.

Our words scoop up more than they can hold.

I get so sad to think of this and how it will feel to lose you.

It's as if these are facts, or you'd lost your mind.

Your last moment of consciousness is nowhere but in the way the bits of a yellow light show through the moving branches of snow-covered trees.

Everything is worthy of our attention.

You speak of taking the poem to bed, living on the internet or in your girl's desires.

I am that girl.

I want to turn my neediness into greater self-sufficiency, but when I'm happy, I want to be happier still.

I have tiny lightning bolts in a bowl for breakfast, one hundred and twenty states of consciousness and then some straight, clean, four AM lines.

Sometimes I change.

I'm the collection pool you pass through on your way to the store.

I almost can't bear this feeling and I'm not feeling any "thing."

I am an agitated squirrel without a nut.

I am the conviction of lined paper.

Yes, and some small goods must accumulate before we recognize them as goods at all.

Let me, (you let me), try to shock and hug you in one beat.

You have no system to absorb this drunk, this kick, all smiles and moving mannequins.

You're looking for a rental.

You are a composite yourself.

I rip you out of one book to mark my place in another.

Blue does not describe the book or the boat, but it's part of it.

It's one child.

It's decades and decades.

We receive another soft acceptance and we wear soft clothing.

The Cows

Assertions in the humongous muck you call "complex psychiatric conditions" and I call breezes.

It's like determining market value or lining up for something stupid.

Is it not enough that on top of nothing there is everything?

No information comes or goes.

When I can't think what else to say, I say "Thank you."

Cars pass each other on the highway and that's all.

Seven, then ten, then twelve cows surround me and their circle gets tighter.

Their hovering sharpens the light, and I judge the light's movements, like the cows', by the freshness of its manure.

Do it.

We want the pieces to fit together, but what if?

They don't.

A violin snow in the trees.

She has twins.

Young hands and tea kettles.

Friends, brain meat.

From a name word to a squiggle line, a thigh, a slow-down.

A crater, a phone, a war in the distance, tiger, the back of your wife, the wife on your back, watercolor bridge.

Now you can hold the bottoms of your feet before your eyes.

You are literally coming apart.

Your love life, your collection, your assumptions run wild.

And what the wild animals do while you do this.

The doctor, the dying, the sleep within.

The challenge of keeping the characters straight when they are merely intended as vessels for the message.

Or is the fiction a fib?

Cause and effect complicated.

A man is sick, a woman is sick, a bird dies, a hand waves.

If it's all one.

Sit on my hat, why don't you?

the frank and pitying gaze

I take my class outside to dig holes.

It's ridiculous how enthusiastic I am.

This gladness inhibits any further exploration until another
exploration becomes an equal gladness.

Where do my edges meet your logic?

You say, "Fuck the casual reader."

It's the nature of the global moment, a paper-bag brown, a knock-out
blue, creamy creaminess.

Horizons go vertical.

In the Horses' Sun

There's good reason not to mix it together.

Your mother is still alive.

She comes out of the bath like a reflection.

Relative to you, she's upside down.

We could say you love each other or at least you are interested in each other.

Everyone flaps in the wind.

The deer hanging in McGuirk's barn is not what we call living.

The elastic tense quickly morphs into a big fat lie.

Our Bravado

Dreading the dreading is worse than the dreading.

Mood doesn't matter.

Sequencing is arbitrary.

Every sum is different.

If you believe wholeheartedly in doubt, well then, you know what I'm talking about.

I'm not saying anything.

When humans visited earth, everyone desired and then mended and then desired again.

You were my snowman and my beekeeper and my oxygen mask.

High ceilings, terraces, cocktail patios, and justice worked.

This is one funny day full of defeated characters and one undefeated one.

I've counted sixteen principles of sunshine.

We pile into our double bubble maps.

This is a public art that ignores the public.

Your name is on the list of names.

I want to point you away from this.

Parrot Tulip Ground African Taffy Iris

Lime Prussian Venetian smashing French perfect

Wave mighty electric morning Utah royal

Windmill pale wings crocus colonial rose

Oyster silken fog reef borrowed glow

Glory ink slipper bath sheep pavilion

Seed pocket string splash mushroom hollow

Hound bamboo creek board cement grass

Down butter pipe stone bird evening

Sassy puddle middle floor master bound

Vacation carpet yolk air bucket leather

Caper closet bottle path leaf barn

Daytime cream ladybug landscape eggshell carry

Olive ice cooks spoons hardware younger

Mud nickel mint pine escapement turtle

Treatment clapboard uplift breakfast smoke flannel

Tint peacock spring booth camel robin

Moss mood crest blanch flesh faith

Camera cold grain thousand boat hut

Tissue infant raspberry sunflower water slate

Guest horse pressure Jamaica earring omelet

Shoulder departure afternoon wall syrup nail

Neutral ruby steak lipstick alarm bracket

Paprika candle charcoal cool trick park

Polish honey dark misty coat blaze

Buff tea tone ash turf block

English mess carbon stripe drink lamp

Under east brush enamel attitude

Vintage skipper cupid milk interior relay

Flour both mute shower function fabric

Shine mahogany law bath gimmick oil

Dry Florida produce care wool mustard

Exterior guest glass key snap sex

Ache almond towel cactus coral apparition

Shade tender kind particular foot envelope

World napkin fear shard box pastry

Alligator yam brass hip distinguish chutney

Jump giraffe architecture expedition carnation pepper

Acoustics

You eat in a crowded restaurant.

You drag your clothes across the public floor.

You don't make comparisons.

You take a break from comparisons.

A voice whisper-calls, "Hey Lesle."

Meanwhile

It looks easy to write for love, water, and love.

This happens and then this and then things stop.

That's the plot.

Our placentas detach.

Our placebos have side effects.

We are brothers and sisters with conflicting theories.

Do we contradict the given?

Frequently sacrifice the comprehensible to the unfathomable?

To the suffering of centuries?

Is earth to hold the plants?

In Every Square

She's afraid of overcoats in her dream.

One for you and one for you.

Because she has to.

Two horses and one boat.

The "I" card falls first in the rain.

Your woes will be brief.

Orange, the fruit.

Meanwhile, the cattle and boulders hunch in the field.

This is your state of drifting in the sunset bus.

And these are the physical properties of matter and mattering.

No pictures of the high-heeled trucks and the book drums or the pineapple town or rabbit pipe or fish chain.

Not smoke, but about smoke.

We take the bridge to pieces.

On the other side, people are bigger or there are no people.

How far can a conceptual sphere stretch before it pops?

Analogy making lies at the heart of pattern perception and extrapolation.

Elegance and consistency unravel a sample sequence.

Happiness and urgency are deeply intertwined, and they combine to yield a total outcome that is the overall behavior of the system.

It can happen that these voices momentarily cross each other, or in some other manner wind up playing the same note, so that for a brief period it would be impossible to disentangle them from each other if the passage were heard in isolation, out of context.

Answers of this sort remind us a bit of the famous old nine-dot puzzle.

Uninjured Things

The first phase of the occupation was chaotic, an eye for bad things
 as modest as these landscape canvases may have seemed.

Without the intrusion of self, ostensibly mined raw feeling pleases
too easily.

The transforming moment is when the second stage of the process
selectively reinforces or diminishes the first stage.

No motif, only motivation.

It did leave a residue, a plural, as unsettling.

This last point bears reiteration and amplification, rather than lament.

In the Cemetery of the Dead and Singing Birds

The dead do not depend on us and their conversations are dull.

Small fish flop and expire around vernal pools.

Our digestion hurts.

We write a BUY MILK note and bring money.

There is always more missing information than given.

What's given turns out to be between things.

We drop off some needs and add a bee buzz.

We stand in the lakes.

We disappear in a pop.

Despite our best intentions, it is not honest to call ourselves "other."

We punch someone in the nose and wait to be punched back.

A wooden pear rolls across the highway.

We play cards and drink tea under the mangroves.

The Coat Room

Wreckage: I'm sorry I said what I said at lunch.

Non-Boolean: I am interested in seeing everything.

I need not to continue: a device that can alter the magnitude of a force is a useful machine.

The fish and the circle: "to brood in the deep."

Metaphor: same problem, different body.

Front and back: without you, there would be no me.

Time on a train: I don't want to be a cause of pain or a person worthy of disdain.

Density and destiny: enjoyment and employment.

Navigating the escalators: finding the coat room.

The memory-imagination continuum: I forgot to tell you that Patrick died.

How many months until spring: how many mouths do you have?

It turns out: I inherited the ability to swallow many pills at once.

Condensation: if we name it, we separate it from its larger existence and we call it Bruce.

The timely application of skepticism: there's no reason to add a layer to see what will happen and there's no reason not to add a layer.

The sun makes triangles with the buildings: my middle, kiss, name.

Mood: a silk curtain over the sea.

Two headaches: eggs.

There is no audience, no conclusion: the bridge might get longer for its reaching.

To find love for yourself: field after field, wild fruit, snipes and woodcocks.

Rain, Birds, Amendment

A circular frame goes around us and touches itself where it started, but ending where it started does not make it a circle.

We have a grave self-consciousness unencumbered, perhaps too unencumbered.

We'll find our luggage eventually.

Things are going to happen now.

A big wave flattens us face down in the sand.

It passes and we stand up and everything is all right again, but there's lots to clean up, many dead fish.

Is our path too narrow?

Will we come back the same way?

I have a good middle-term memory

I have many husbands.

You are a human being with a brain on a couch in a house.

The busyness of your interior has become a dense wet green.

We wade through the tall deer grass, remove our boots and wade into the swamp to gather fairy mist together.

As the morning grows, we get rid of a lot of nonsense.

Where we go deep we could drop more things, but there's no thinking away what the future philosophers might think which will be based on future science.

The body is a problem, maybe a good one, but still a problem.

We walk away midsentence.

We misread pain and medication as poem and meditation.

Our shoulders twitch like lupines in the wind, buttercups, and hawkweed.

It's brighter.

I mean better.

I have a stinging tongue.

We're getting somewhere.

Our guests sleep, but we're awake and vigilant.

We develop a sentence theory of.

Our book is.

Our hair long.

We feel better.

Sometimes I can't bear your beauty.

How often do you regret acts of impulsivity and is that regret great enough?

What convictions have hummingbirds in heaven?

Frequently we make turns automatically.

We find ourselves we don't know where, but there's a new dirt on our floor.

The good and bad behind us might be equal to the good and bad ahead.

Might we rearrange the lawn furniture to be happy, or at least happier?

It's like a cake with layers of difficulty and layers of pleasure and eventually losing everything we love.

We hold a dying monarch in our hands and put her down on the sill of the shed.

What if the feeling is real, but maybe not true outside of its owner?

The shade comes after us.

Our brains loop around and around looking for the image to ground the idea.

We can't breathe.

Then the Sunoco sign.

Then we wake up.

The river runs fast in the channel and the sun pours onto it so you document it.

Sometimes it's like a pair of glasses and a hearing aid that ups it all.

You bake yourself flat.

Everything it took to get here, and nothing can be done with it.

Nonsentences don't help us and sentences are never complete and water so flat and still and you are, I tell you, solid upon it, my author, my peony, my cupcake, my condition, my young one, my pillow.

At night in our insomniac boats, we hold ten foot long brushes and make easy sweeps on the ceilings.

Coming or going we have to leap the drainage ditch either way.

We are space-takers like clothes hung on a limited line.

When we leave, the absences slide in.

Albert is depressed, Fiona heartbroken, Plaatsburg philosophical.

I busy myself with kitchen tasks.

And when you say this and that, do you mean this reminds you of that feeling?

Is the sun returning?

The dog vomiting?

Am I lonely for my brothers?

Mud runs through the freight yards.

We find a party.

We are unsure with glitter on our feet.

We wait on the line we draw.

We put out a chair.

We sit in the rotunda.

Until the relationships between objects become clearer, you will probably think things are happening to you.

You watch rain fall on the surface of the vacuum.

What you've called sadness is only a superficial form of it.

World form is a speck in it.

There are many written word removal systems but only apologies for the spoken.

Prove me wrong.

I wish it was hard-covered.

I wish this was an objective situation like the water-holding limitations of a lake.

If I say this, if I name you, I bring you down.

Your death is the man on the road without a car or a man without a car on the road.

In the Inn

I didn't and didn't sleep.

I hung between random events and a linear life.

Guests walked their dogs through the big room lobby.

You told me the earth moves and I told you it all moves.

Kids swished by in ski pants.

Drinkers clinked glasses in the bar.

This adds up.

It's like a robot of love, an old boyfriend, I mean really old.

The clerks talk sports.

Then the director shoots himself.

Mathematical proofs prove abstractions.

Emergency Horse

drabness racer elephant light iron Dutch show folly studio coast dance
biscuit cooking northbound morning saddle leap saucer help atrium
checker booth plum lightweight

opera daybreak Dakar cancer plain gestation insect whistle cheese police
youth infestation communication triple cremation stomp token peanut
figure

escape witness triangular bandana crankcase underneath bonding crepes
stars figurine attempt poultry forgery freak tank study

eyeball guppy suit stem invention coral instant pile sibling gravity theatre
Paris cut snore banquet

luck awake purgatory purchase book injury seacoast terrain uncle
eventually climb philanthropy

surgery freeze bag collapse windfall insurgence fire anticipate girl
inevitable square eclipse warning double

caution sidewalk vest nurse washcloth wagon tundra blood pace devil
plus baseball pulse Olympic remainder mustache practice meeting
injection pattern

athletic winsome sandy waiting hallway wetland wingnut grief animal gift

telephone holiday historic

Work on Paper

Red Sea Scarf

Be sharp man and soar. Brain head globes for nothing. The cut language yanks the red sea scarf and shoot it. We don't clean up the mess because we want to see it be it free it.

Blue

Woman it's time the waiting and ready time. And we'll slip and fall. Be a worry sandwich on dream bread. Baby Mary Emma dies. Cold is good. It drips down and eats you just to put where you are down. A train trip through the forest of moods left behind.

Red 2

All of you givens and the light's out a crime a dime a lemon burger. Everyone in the family hotel interplay it works in clay ground fantastic elastic surround more ground sound. In an open state of oscillation we play multiple parts, dive into the fast current with daylight jumping all over it in first crazy time. We know you had company. It was a drive by on the byway whatever I say.

Yellow 2

We touch a flash of a life of love. 83. First person's discovered. Silent reading's discovered. Up to 1,000. Avenue what you call. We build up to this. Just this? Flat town the dead.

Y

Broken Open Flood. Temple Attendance. Done. Sitting on the Fence. A Bird. Drinking Your Way Down. Perfect.

Another Another

The goodness has collapsed and gone.

It's the same "now" for everyone.

We are at onceness at oneness.

We are a long march of people and resources, waves and sheep, a march of demonstratives.

We eat candy and irony.

Deerhunters roam the woods and bad people are in power.

Good people are digging up reasons not to seek substance-fueled escapes, happier imaginations.

They are walking with their bundles away from the core of the hearts of their enemies.

Their bundles are made of children and cats and dogs and cows and chickens and tigers and elephants and giraffes and sloths and orangutans and alligators and lobsters and spiders and trout and chickadees.

Their bundles are made of what they are without and also the bundles of the others and the others themselves.

One person walks one way, another another.

One person looks one way, another another.

One person thinks up an experiment of entangled particles under the superluminal.

One person simplifies but they limit and deny by simplification, milk, and eggs.

They generalize and share the weather.

Enter the wolf, the toothpick, the bee, the glass, the staircase.

Enter the elite and the ordinary and the back-to-bedders.

One person reads what one writer writes about another writer writing about unfitness.

Enter the superpowers and siblings, the notes to self and accidents.

Meanwhile, until the big hand is on the nine, polarities are stretched farther and no amount of force on one side can break the other.

One person breathes one way, another another.

The people keep their heads down and walk slowly until they are dead and don't carry anything.

Just say "basket" or "no basket," and there's the basket.

The Fallacies of the Misplaced

1.
Labor sight candy
Right situation impeccable
Stationary station pullet

2.
Confidence cloudy tea
Flight bean company
Thickness folder cart

3.
Ballet crow caucus
Velcro turnstile secrete
Fulcrum pajamas slip

4.
Humid triangle particular
Wife step report
Tomorrow mist frozen

5.
River hot quarter
Double institution key
Crisp reflection start

6.
Moth shore small
Trinket botany bay
Stop storm man

7.
Negative style bear
Square maple fanning
Mall age scene

8.
Proof symptom carpenter
Silly saw cure
Walking coast over

9.
Mere inflate worker
Jester motherly bauble
Resting pull flooring

10.
Cheek haggle continuous
Addiction medium pour
Mealtime name torture

11.
Exposure fools manifest
Greed way discussion
Field fear tear

12.
Silk remote bead
Farfetched second fig
Position swap consider

13.
Drape temple size
Yarn cubicle coal
Greek electric dark

14.
Radical absorption fact
Starve diagnose profuse
Planned sky bark

15.
Scrap assembly pan
Torque scramble insist
Sculpture prevention resistance

16.
Insomnia mop cactus
Lover moisture illumination
Flux streambed global

17.
Humble butter stripes
Peony whispering glacier
Mentor traffic salvage

18.
Execution measure model
Clash standpoint saint
Armchair torch facts

19.
Volcano uniform sister
Harbor inhabit between
Zinc respect prospect

20.
Bounty rival song
Vacuum strict fantastic
Chord friction panorama

21.
Pistol froth error
Opportunity urban wedding
Wet interest intensity

22.
Effort morning meander
Cow recycle busy
Breast inherit news

23.
Lawn lakefront Maxwell
Overcast headline post
Other angle sting

24.
Prey drinking industry
Relative hidden twitter
Kingfisher sign Rhinebeck

25.
Flat rag leaf
Sorrow chain rock
Afternoon wish fraught

26.
Tax soup mirror
Wander crestfallen stand
Generous town cleaning

27.
Bleeding forgetting ownership
Yours camp cover
Quarantine white ladder

Lunchtime

You put your umbrella in the car and leave your car in the parking lot and lock the car and later go back to the car to get your umbrella but forget your keys and it's raining.

You don't push the bad things off but let them break off on their own.

It's not true that only like things can be added.

It's okay if in the total collapse of meaning, this is the temperature.

We continue adding until the excess lessens itself.

It's a big fat bird call.

Water comes out of our guns.

Our currency is defunct.

When no one needs us, we need ourselves.

We use every bit of what we have.

In Tulip and Bird City, Ohio, where is Henry?

He isn't here.

It's just us.

Our papers stick out over the edge of the table.

At least we have a table.

Our dreamy cookie baker never stops talking.

Did I forget to say that we are white?

How are our minds not blown away?

Have we fallen into the sea or into psychedelics?

Our shapes fall unlit.

Our shadows fall on a boat, a newspaper, garbage, an egg, a field, a fish, a school, a neck, a highway, New England, a herd of cows along a snaking river.

Sun pours on the river, opens us and breaks us.

Love eats us up.

You say that south is down from here.

I anticipate your departure.

I act cheerful as if cheerfulness were here.

I become this gladly flying sock shape.

"I will not let you have the weapons that I have."

Thank you very much, but no.

I say no to happiness for something better.

But where is Chicken Bridge?

Where the chicken truck crashed.

We drive to Sally's and have lunch.

The space between us is quiet, like a village of butterflies.

We stand on separate triangle peaks.

We move our palms up and down weighing the air.

The world without us is a mood flat on the horizon.

What's in our kitchen pot?

The Great Temple of Love in Bridgeport.

Our hearts are yanked out.

If we break our pills in half, we can have two good days.

If we dig down deep enough, we come up with real hope—if we can come up.

We hope the tractor won't break down.

We hope the crops grow.

We pray the dams won't displace the villages.

The air is slippery.

Please don't give me anything else to think about before bed or I'll think about it.

I don't care if nothing holds it all together.

I'm in my big-girl bed.

I look over valley and hills and try to account for other lives.

Infinity goes in every direction.

We piece together a diagram.

We live in the midst of desire.

When desire finds its language it's as relieving as finding a lost dog.

If he ran off to eat deer guts, that's what he did.

Our lives can change, will change, in a second, any second.

Whoever is drinking a martini.

You are beginning, just beginning, to wish you were wearing clothes.

You sing to yourself.

You are lovely, stretched, imagined.

I don't get tired of looking at you, so battered and proud, classic, hopeful, full of garlic and mountains.

The grass is pushing the limits of green.

Other people are walking around.

I feel porous.

The big birch drips its buds.

The boy duck quacks for his girl.

Here's a beetle, a hundred dollars, a shell, a muffin.

Here is the bridge out and what's left of it that's not symbolic.

Here is the time it takes your medicine to work.

Here is the sound of the leaves sliding out of their slippery cases.

Here is the fallout, the falcon, the corpse, the splash of animal.

Everything is ragged.

You should come home.

Here is an improvisational water rat.

Here are farm women dreaming of fire engines.

Here's a bucketful of large eggs, a house of goats, a hot geranium, astronauts flying over highways, kitchens in rabbit holes, bodies made of clay.

Here is a road to walk which connects to another and heads into town, then out of town.

We blast out.

We have no obstacles.

How many poems?

Nine.

How many moons?

Two.

How many boyfriends?

Three.

A thought with all its parts separated is spread out on the ground before us.

It weighs seven pounds and slides over flat rocks.

This is the bright red wet cut end.

This is like sitting by a waterfall or an open state of minding.

A sheep hovers over the text.

A house sits on the text.

A man sits on the house.

Tonight Jupiter, Mars, and Saturn are visible.

Your bedroom is a restaurant.

Your train is off its track.

Your dog is better than your notebook.

What gold do you carry in your pollen baskets?

What kind of truck do you drive?

We are little people on the surface of a planet.

This is an unflat and interesting planet.

This is an edge of grasping nature and void.

If you are a wind in the world, I am a breeze.

Life is like a breeze.

Here is an unsanded sharp corner.

This barely-a-path ends in the cemetery.

Here lie Elmer and Madeline and Lou and Marianne.

I'm talking about the clouds here.

They look like a mouth, no a moth, no a mouth.

The mouth is a heart.

The thumping heart of the phoebe bird says, "Be happy."

"Be calm."

"Be efficient."

"Be on time."

"Be willing."

"Be loving."

"Be sleeping."

"Be working."

"Be kind to others, the earth, and the animals."

She looks through the bin of socks.

There is no meaning, but "Be cheerful."

"Be quiet."

"Be thoughtful."

"Be useful."

How thirsty are we?

How thirsty we are!

If this is the situation, this is the hum of the iguana.

This is the situation.

The snowflakes fall as quietly as periods holding hands.

Conversations are expectations to meet or disappoint.

We don't know whether to say the right thing or say it right.

Little did you know and little do I.

Your imagination is a painful organ.

A live bird pecks at a dead one.

You ask me life or death questions, but I can't think—I mean at all.

I must be incomplete if there is also this milk jug.

The wheat through the window and the pig puffy clouds pass.

Butcher the pig.

Hang the clothes.

Go to the bar.

Meet the woman with her skeleton girlfriend.

You sit on the stone stoop because why not?

Your friends cannot explain themselves with themselves.

And if they could, what would be the reason?

You think it's fine to be extravagant with yourself, but it's not.

Your privilege has a spreading impact.

What you relinquish to live without fear is too much.

Did you leave room for anything else?

No one says you can do whatever you want.

At least this is your psychiatrist's stance.

You're not just willing.

You are eager to explore the roads grown over around the abandoned farm fields, under the electric fence barriers, over the wetlands, through gates to open and close, through tall tick grass, over hilly cow pastures, to the old oaks to sit under.

That's all you have to do.

You buy into the ongoingness.

You confess everything.

Your nerves also hum.

You don't know how to put it together.

There's no way to do it.

We have only the desire to do a little bit of nothing and nothing more.

We visit Mary and Asa Dearth.

Then Enoch who is by himself.

We drive over pink wax hills.

Plastic flowers grow.

We visit Thedora.

We eat dinner at Black Bear Tavern.

We are quiet as small buddhas on green museum grounds in the rain.

We stay at Northern Comfort Motel on Route 3 in Colebrook.

We don't need to plan.

What's ahead comes at us anyway.

I try to be as good as you are at not complaining.

Do you want half my cake?

I want to be more giving.

Do you want my whole cake?

We spend long hours in isolated landscapes like two birds in one tree and it's spring and we are free of our paying jobs.

There is a cherry orchard.

Even if every new moment includes the loss of the last, we host a momentary good mood fairy.

I don't know more than you do about this even if I'm in it, and if less is more, more is also more.

I know less.

These are the odds.

We hear November's hunters' guns, chainsaws, and terrible, terrible news.

When will it be okay again and will it?

We've divided ourselves in order to see more multidirectionality.

If we are unhappy merely because we are not happy, we should be able to talk ourselves around.

What we think is for sure, the aluminum thing on wheels, is not for sure.

We never have a minute without an expectation.

We accumulate, release, suffer increased accumulation.

NOTES

"How far can a conceptual sphere stretch before it pops?" is composed of excerpts from *Fluid Concepts and Creative Analogies* by Daniel Hofstadter.

"Uninjured Things" is composed of excerpts from *Doubt and Belief in Painting* by Richard Storr.

ACKNOWLEDGMENTS

The author is grateful to the editors of the following journals in whose pages some of these poems first appeared, sometimes in earlier versions: *Massachusetts Review, jubilat, Spoke Too Soon, Bodega, Truck, Ping Pong, New World Writing, Third Coast, Paperbag, Cold Mountain Review, Fence,* and *Body.*

Also by **Lesle Lewis**

Small Boat

Landscapes I & II

lie down too

A Boot's a Boot

It's Rothko in Winter or Belgium.

The Ottoline Prize, previously incarnated as the Motherwell Prize and the Alberta Prize, is an annual series, generously endowed by Jennifer S. Epstein, offering publication to a second book of poems or greater by a woman, a five thousand dollar cash prize, and a residency at Eliot House, in Gloucester, MA. Past winners include Chelsey Minnis, Harmony Holiday, Sasha Steensen, Laura Sims, Stacy Szymaszek, Wendy Xu, and Ariana Reines.

For more about this and other Fence activities visit fenceportal.org.